To Helen, Evelyn and Belle

Parent's Introduction

We Both Read is the first series of books designed to invite parents and children to share the reading of a story by taking turns reading aloud. This "shared reading" innovation, which was developed with reading education specialists, invites parents to read the more complex text and storyline on the left-hand pages. Children are encouraged to read the right-hand pages, which feature less complex text and storyline, specifically written for the beginning reader.

Reading aloud is one of the most important activities parents can share with their child to assist them in their reading development. However, *We Both Read* goes beyond reading *to* a child and allows parents to share the reading *with* a child. *We Both Read* is so powerful and effective because it combines two key elements in learning: "modeling" (the parent reads) and "doing" (the child reads). The result is not only faster reading development for the child, but a much more enjoyable and enriching experience for both!

You may find it helpful to read the entire book aloud yourself the first time, then invite your child to participate in the second reading. In some books, a few more difficult words will first be introduced in the parent's text, distinguished with **bold lettering**. Pointing out, and even discussing, these words will help familiarize your child with them and help to build your child's vocabulary. Also, note that a "talking parent" icon ⓖ precedes the parent's text and a "talking child" icon ⓒ precedes the child's text.

We encourage you to share and interact with your child as you read the book together. If your child is having difficulty, you might want to mention a few things to help them. "Sounding out" is good, but it will not work with all words. Children can pick up clues about the words they are reading from the story, the context of the sentence, or even the pictures. Some stories have rhyming patterns that might help. It might also help them to touch the words with their finger as they read, to better connect the voice sound and the printed word.

Sharing the *We Both Read* books together will engage you and your child in an interactive adventure in reading! It is a fun and easy way to encourage and help your child to read—and a wonderful way to start them off on a lifetime of reading enjoyment!

We Both Read: When I Grow Up

———————————————————

We Both Read® is a trademark of Treasure Bay, Inc.

Published by Treasure Bay, Inc.
40 Sir Francis Drake Blvd.
San Anselmo, CA 94960 USA

PRINTED IN SINGAPORE

Library of Congress Control Number: 2004112172

Hardcover ISBN: 1-891327-57-7
Paperback ISBN: 1-891327-58-5

05 06 07 08 09 / 10 9 8 7 6 5 4 3 2

We Both Read® Books
Patent No. 5,957,693

Visit us online at:
www.webothread.com

WE BOTH READ ®

When I Grow Up

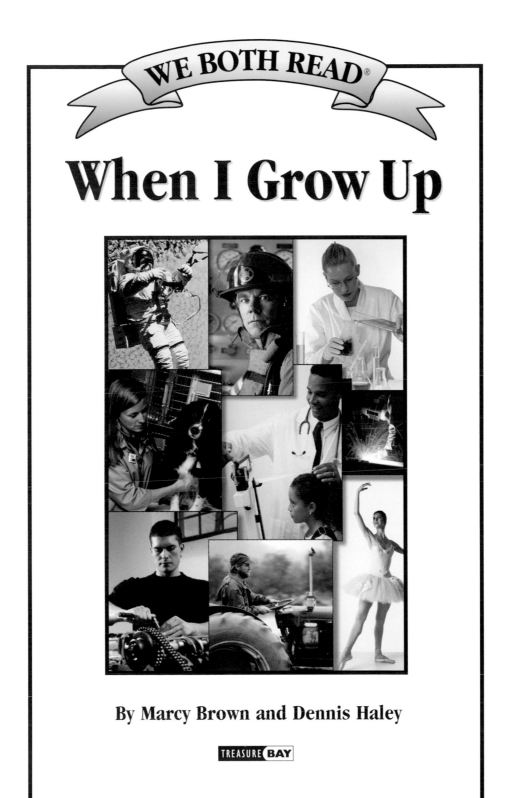

By Marcy Brown and Dennis Haley

TREASURE BAY

What do you want to be when you **grow** up? Maybe you'd like to be a doctor. Or you could be a painter. How about a homemaker? There are so many choices!

Think about the things you enjoy doing right now. One of those things could turn into a job you love when you **grow** up.

These girls love ice cream.
They could make ice cream
when they **grow** up.

2

 Maybe you like digging and pretending that you're at the wheel of a big **backhoe** or a powerful **bulldozer**. Backhoes and bulldozers are often used when a house is being built. The backhoe digs up the earth and the bulldozer moves the dirt out of the way.

Which one would you like to drive? A **bulldozer** or a **backhoe**? You could drive both!

It takes a lot of people to build a house. An architect makes a drawing of what the house will look like. Then the construction workers build the floors and walls and roof. Once the outside of the house is built, a new group of people start to work on the inside. Carpenters put in floors and cabinets. **Painters** paint the walls and ceilings.

Oops! Maybe this man should not be a **painter**. Can you see why?

If you like cats, dogs and turtles, you might someday grow up to be a veterinarian. A veterinarian is a doctor for animals.

A veterinarian looks in an animal's ears and listens to its heart to be sure it is healthy. They may have to give a shot to make it feel **better**.

A hug can also make a pet feel **better**.

Do you sometimes like to just sit and wonder? Why does a soft drink have so many bubbles? What makes some balloons go up when you let go of them? How does water change from a liquid into a solid ice cube?

If wondering is your kind of fun, you could be a **scientist**!

👓 A **scientist** helped this man go into space. Scientists can also go into space!

Maybe you would like to be a homemaker when you grow up. Homemakers work in the home, **taking care** of the house and the **family**. Some of their many responsibilities include cooking, cleaning, shopping, and **taking care** of all the little emergencies that can happen in a **family**.

Taking care of a home and a **family** is a big job. Moms can do it and dads can too!

12

   Did you know it is someone's job to write the things that you read and watch on TV? The people who write these things are called **writers**.

Writers write books and magazines. They also write newspapers, cookbooks, television shows, comic books and more.

Two **writers** wrote this book!

If you like to draw or paint, you could be an artist someday.

There are many ways to create art. Some artists use paint and paper. Artists who use clay or stone to make art are called sculptors. Some artists even use scissors to make their art!

Do you think this is art?
This boy thinks it is.

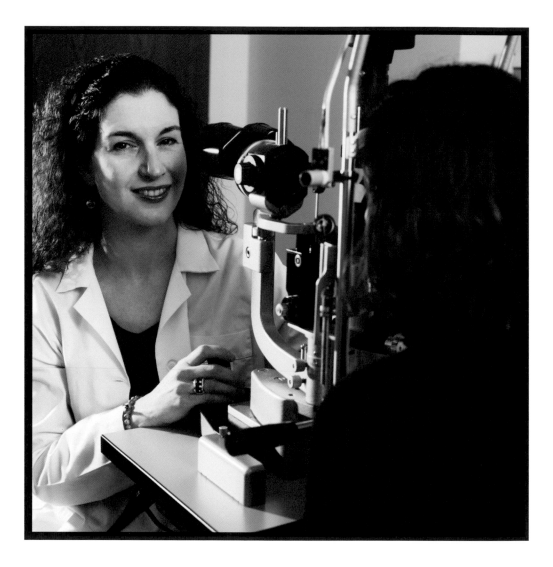

 This lady is an ophthalmologist—an **eye** doctor.

When she was a little girl, an ophthalmologist helped her to see better and that made her so happy that she decided to become an ophthalmologist too. But first she had to learn how to spell it!

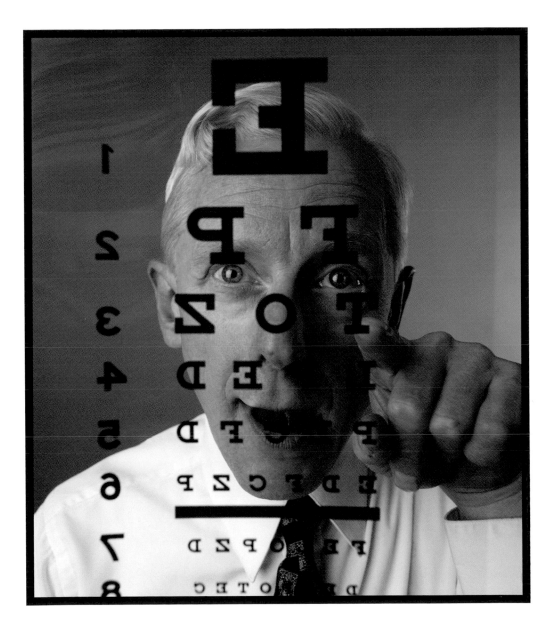

This man is taking an eye test. This test may help him to see better.

Teachers give tests too. They also give homework! But they do much more than that. **Teachers** help young people **learn** to read and write and work with numbers and so much more.

Kids can be **teachers** too. You can help someone **learn**. It's fun!

What if your favorite thing to do is to play on the beach and go swimming in the water? You could grow up to be a lifeguard. **Lifeguard**s watch people in and out of the water.

👓 **Lifeguards** are there to make sure you are safe.

   Have you ever sold lemonade in your front yard? If you have, you might just have the makings for a career in sales.

There are many different kinds of sales people. Some sell clothes. Some sell houses. Some sell insurance. And some sell lemonade.

23

This woman sells houses. She helps people find just the right house. That makes them very happy.

 Working on a farm is a very **important** job. Farmers grow the food that we eat. They can grow fruit or vegetables or both. Some farmers get to drive big tractors.

 Growing food is very **important**. But some kids like to play with food. And some kids like to cook food.

 If you like cooking, you could be a chef someday!

A chef knows how to prepare lots of different foods to create delicious meals. A chef who makes breads and cakes is called a baker. A pastry chef makes sweet, fluffy, crunchy desserts. Yum!

What if you like to be silly?
Is there a job for you?

Yes! Clowns are silly! Clowns make people laugh and feel good. Clowns work at birthday parties and circuses and some visit hospitals. There is even a school for clowns. Being a clown is an important job because people need to laugh.

This girl has fun talking on the phone. She could do it all day long.

   Working as a customer service representative is one job that is all about talking on the telephone. Most businesses have representatives who talk to the customers who have questions or problems. These people are friendly and helpful. And they get to talk on the phone all day long.

This boy loves music. What kind of job could he do?

 There are many possible careers for music lovers. A composer writes music for others to play. A musician plays the music on an instrument. A recording engineer records music and a disc jockey plays music on the radio. Teaching other people about music is also a great job.

Do you like to fix things?

If you like using tools and fixing things, there are many jobs for you.

You could be a mechanic and repair cars or airplanes or motorcycles. You could be a computer technician and repair computers. Plumbers and electricians repair things in your home.

As long as things keep breaking, there will be a job for you!

 Jets are cool! Would you like to fly one?

If you like jets and would like to travel all over the world, being an airline pilot just might be the job for you.

Airline pilots fly jet **airplanes** that **deliver** people and cargo to destinations around the world. "Cargo" is a fancy word for all the supplies and goods that need to be flown from one place to another.

This box came off of an **airplane**. Now this man will **deliver** it. That is his job.

38

There are more kinds of jobs than you could ever imagine. People working at jobs build the things we need, help us to stay healthy, entertain us, and affect our lives in so many ways. There is even a job to tell people about the kinds of jobs there are.

So what do YOU want to
do when you grow up?

If you liked
***When I Grow Up*, here are two other**
***We Both Read*® Books you are sure to enjoy!**

This simple Level 1 book explores the seasons through the changing weather and the changing activities of both children and animals. There is a brief description of why the earth has four seasons, but most of the book is devoted to the delightful new world that each season brings into our life.

To see all the We Both Read books that are available,
just go online to **www.webothread.com**

Featuring delightful photographs, this book explores
the wonderful world of both popular and unusual
pets. In simple language, it discusses the joys, as well
as the responsibilities, of pet ownership. This book is
sure to be a hit with everyone who has, or even wishes
they could have, a pet.